Gastric Band & Deep Sleep Hypnosis:

Positive Affirmations & Guided Meditations
For Rapid Weight Loss, Self-Love &
Extreme Fat Burn+ Overcoming Insomnia,
Body Anxiety & Overthinking

© Copyright 2021 - All rights reserved.

The content contained within this book may not be reproduced, duplicated or transmitted without direct written permission from the author or the publisher.

Under no circumstances will any blame or legal responsibility be held against the publisher, or author, for any damages, reparation, or monetary loss due to the information contained within this book; either directly or indirectly.

Legal Notice:

This book is copyright protected. This book is only for personal use. You cannot amend, distribute, sell, use, quote or paraphrase any part, or the content within this book, without the consent of the author or publisher.

Disclaimer Notice:

Please note the information contained within this document is for educational and entertainment purposes only. All effort has been executed to present accurate, up to date, and reliable, complete information. No warranties of any kind are declared or implied. Readers acknowledge that the author is not engaging in the rendering of legal, financial, medical or professional advice.

In this 10-hour series, we explore weight loss and deep sleep, naturally, through guided hypnosis, meditation and affirmations.

This audiobook will include a series of hypnotherapy sessions, guided meditations and affirmations, that will transform the hearts and minds of listeners who are desperately seeking ways to lose weight and combat insomnia.

All sessions are original content, written by a qualified Hypnotherapist with extensive experience in helping people achieve their personal life goals naturally.

The Sessions

The sessions will unfold as follows:

Session 1: Hypnosis Script - Deep Sleep 13

Session 2: Hypnosis Script - Body Anxiety & Overthinking 32

Session 3: Hypnosis Script – Fat Burn & Exercise 49

Session 4: Hypnosis Script – Self-love & Integration 66

Session 5: Guided Meditation - Overcoming Insomnia 87

Session 6: Guided Meditation - Self Love & Weight Loss 102

Session 7: Guided Meditation - Deep Sleep For Rapid Weight Loss 120

Session 5: Affirmations - Overcoming Insomnia 139

Session 6: Affirmations - Extreme fat burn.144

Session 7: Affirmations - Overcoming Body Anxiety 149

Conclusion 154

Introduction:

About this Audiobook.

Hello and welcome to Weight Loss and Deep Sleep a 10-hr Audiobook, brought to you by _____ This powerful 10-hour series will provide you with powerful hypnosis to induce a natural and deep sleep every night and to achieve your ideal weight by working on self-image, exercise and fat burning naturally for rapid transformation!

Weight Loss and Deep Sleep is a series of powerful hypnosis audios, and transformational guided meditations, designed to unleash your mental capacity to drop the pounds, shed the fat fast and sleep well while doing it! There are also three bonus affirmation audios created especially for you to listen to on a daily basis to accelerate your weight loss journey!

Each session has been made using powerful hypnotherapeutic techniques to work on the limiting beliefs, resistances, lack of exercise and remove the blocks you hold to weight loss and overcoming insomnia easily.

Who this audiobook is suitable for

This audiobook is open for all who wish to lose weight, attain their weight goals and have trouble sleeping.

What results you can expect

This audiobook is very powerful and can entirely change one's beliefs, actions, resistances, and behaviours linked to weight loss and deep sleep. Repetition is required in order to gain the full benefits from this powerful process.

How to use this content.

It is recommended that the listener is in a place where they can have at least 30-60 minutes of time to themselves depending on which session is being listened to.

Simply find a place to either sit down or lie down comfortably. It is also recommended that the listener uses earphones or headphones for maximum effect, however they are not entirely necessary.

Session 1. Weight Loss and Deep Sleep: Hypnosis Session - Deep Sleep

Overview:
A 60-min Hypnosis session.
This session will focus on direct suggestions to help the listener fall asleep whenever they go to bed. Including powerful induction deepeners, metaphors, direct suggestions and ego-strengthening.

Session 2. Weight Loss and Deep Sleep: Hypnosis Session - Body Anxiety & Overthinking

Overview:
A 60-min Hypnosis session.

This session will focus on overcoming body anxiety and putting an end to overthinking. The session includes powerful induction, deepeners and the use of a powerful metaphor to overcome body anxiety and overthinking along with direct suggestion and ego-strengthening.

Session 3. Weight Loss and Deep Sleep: Hypnosis Session - Fat Burn & Exercise

Overview:
A 60-min Hypnosis session.

This session will focus on direct suggestions for fat burning and motivation for exercising daily. Includes induction, deepeners, a collection of suggestions to focus on exercise and a metaphor for increased fat burning and ego-strengthening.

Session 4. Weight Loss and Deep Sleep: Hypnosis Session - Self Love and Integration

Overview:
A 60-min Hypnosis session.

This session will focus on reconnecting the listener to self-love by using parts dissociation therapy and sealing off the sessions with self-integration work. Includes induction, deepeners, parts therapy for self-love and self-integration therapy for maintenance and ego-strengthening.

Session 5. Weight Loss and Deep Sleep: Guided Meditation - Overcoming insomnia

Overview:
A 30-min Guided meditation

This guided meditation will focus on addressing our anxieties so that we can release our mind of stress and worries, allowing us to fall into a state of relaxation and to enjoy a deep, uninterrupted sleep.

Session 6. Weight Loss and Deep Sleep: Guided Meditation - Self Love & Weight Loss

Overview:
A 30-min Guided meditation

This guided meditation will focus on embracing self love and acceptance of ourselves. By encouraging self love, we allow ourselves to progress on our weightloss journey, no longer hindered by a belief that we do not deserve a healthy and happy future.

Session 7. Weight Loss and Deep Sleep: Guided Meditation - Deep Sleep for Rapid Weight Loss

Overview:
A 60-min Guided meditation

This meditation will take the listener on a visual journey, guiding them into a state of intense relaxation that will result in a deep sleep and encourage rapid weight loss.

Session 8. Weight Loss and Deep Sleep: Affirmations - Overcoming Insomnia and Weight Loss

Overview:
A 30-min Subliminal affirmation session

This session will include a series of powerful present moment affirmations that will reinforce the reprogramming of the previous hypnotic sessions. These affirmations will focus on the topic of overcoming insomnia.

Session 9. Weight Loss and Deep Sleep: Affirmations - Extreme Fat Burn

Overview:
A 30-min Subliminal affirmation session

This session will include a series of powerful present moment affirmations that will reinforce the reprogramming of the previous hypnotic sessions. These affirmations will focus on the topics of extreme fat burn.

Session 10. Weight Loss and Deep Sleep: Affirmations - Body Anxiety

Overview:

A 30-min Subliminal affirmation session.

This session will include a series of powerful present moment affirmations that will reinforce the reprogramming of the previous hypnotic sessions. These affirmations will focus on the topics of body anxiety.

Session 1: Hypnosis Script - Deep Sleep

Overview: This session will focus on direct suggestions to help the listener fall asleep whenever they go to bed.

Time: 60-minutes

[Reader Notes]

- The rhythm and pace are important therefore please read the following script at a steady pace, ensuring to take your time to guide the listener with your voice.
- Allow long comfortable pauses in between passages that you are happy with, and follow the key set out below to allow longer pauses.
- Embedded commands: Embedded commands will be written in **bold**, the reader must read the bold phrases at a

slightly faster pace than the rest of the script. Eg: "See how easy it is to **Just Relax** Nowww", See how easy it is should be ready normally while "just relax" should be read slightly faster returning back to the normal pace when reading "Nowww".
- Nowww: The word "Nowww" should be emphasized and said on an out-breath as if sighing.

[Pause Key]

… Very short pause: Reader pauses for 2 seconds

/ Short pause: Reader pauses for 10 seconds

// Medium pause: Reader pauses for 20 seconds

/// Long pause: Reader pauses for 30 seconds

[Script Begins]

Welcome to the first session in the Weight-loss and Deep Sleep audiobook! A Hypnosis/Guided Meditation series.

This powerful hypnosis audio will focus on helping you get a good night's rest by working directly with your unconscious mind to induce deep sleep.

Begin by finding a comfortable place where you can be alone for just a little while...

You can either sit down comfortably or lie down, please make sure your arms are by your sides and are uncrossed throughout the session.

Now you are in position, simply allow your eyes to close and imagine a wave of relaxation **travelling down** all the way **down**... from the top of your head to the tips of your toes... as you bring your awareness to your breath simply allow yourself to breathe in healing soothing light that is cleansing your entire body from the top of your head to the tips of your toes... and as you breathe out... allow dirty diseased energy to be exhaled out of your body through your breath... guiding yourself 2 times deeper and deeper... that's right...

And you may hear sounds around you... any sounds inside the room and perhaps you can hear sounds outside the room... how soon will it be before all these sounds will **fade away** into the background... as you disregard these sounds... and allow these sounds to guide you deeper and deeper...

Allowing a wave of descending bliss to take over you... relaxing you more and more... In a moment you will hear me say the word... Nowww and whenever you hear me say the word... Nowww... all the unnecessary nervous tension in your body can... **just relax**... and you can continue to **sink 5 times deeper**... into that wonderful state of peace... that wonderful relaxing state of openness...

So... Nowww... **let go**... drift... float... and descend... deeper and deeper with every word that I say...

And... Nowww... I would like you to imagine a brilliant ball of light floating above your head... this brilliant ball of light has the ability to remove all tension out of anything it comes into contact with... in a moment when I say the word **descend**... I would like you to feel and imagine this ball moving down slowly from the top of your head **down,** relaxing each part of your body that it comes in contact with...

So ready... **descend**... feel and imagine this ball **going down** onto the top of your head... down to your face... relaxing all the muscles in your head and face... and Nowww... allow the ball to **descend further down**... down to your neck and shoulders... allow all the muscles in your neck and shoulders to **just relax**... that's right... Now allowing the ball to expand and **descend down** encompassing your arms and upper chest...allow all the muscles in your arms and chest to simply **relax**... let them become loose and limp...

And... Nowww... allowing the ball to **descend further down** encompassing your abdomen, elbows, hands, and fingers... allow them to relax... **relax completely**...

You're doing really well... allow the ball to **descend down**... into your hips and thighs... allow the muscles of your hips and thighs to simply relax...let them go... loose and limp relaxed...

And Nowww... the ball can **descend** encompassing your knees, shins, and calves... allow these muscles to **relax completely**...

Finally... Nowww... allow the ball to **descend** down to your ankles and feet... allow the ball to relax the muscles of your ankles and feet...Nowww... Very good...

Allow the ball to now **descend down**...**down** through the ground and **all the way down**... into the earth... allowing the earth to reabsorb and reuse this energy for something better... Leaving you with a sense of peace... a sense of calm soothing relaxation ... that's right...

And soon... you will hear me count down from 10 to 1... and with each number I count down from 10 to 1 ...with each descending number you are going 10 times deeper and deeper... so ready...10... Going deeper and deeper...9... Feeling better and better... 8 ... The deeper you go the better you feel... 7... The better you feel the deeper you go... 6... drifting ever more deeper still... and 5... and 4... letting go... 3 ... feeling free... 2... you are almost there... and...1...

Remain deeply relaxed... staying deeply relaxed... I would like to speak with your unconscious mind about a matter of importance... important to you...
And...Nowww... I would like your unconscious mind, the part of you that has the answer to all problems... the part of you that has access to all parts of you... to go searching within yourself for the part of you that is preventing sleep.

And I would like your unconscious mind to bring this part out and float it above your left hand...

/

Notice what this part may look like... perhaps it has a sound... or perhaps it has a feeling... or maybe even all three... however **this part manifests to you** now... become aware of it for a moment...

//

We shall refer to this part as the problem part... I would like you to now ask this problem part for insight as to what it is really doing for you...why is it really here... take a moment to interact with this part in this way Nowww...

//

Nowww... let this part know... that whatever this part needs to **easily sleep all night** now... there is another part of you that has exactly what this part needs to **easily sleep all night** now...

//

Let this part know that you will now go searching for the part of you that has exactly what that part needs to **easily sleep all night**...

//

So Nowww... I would like you to thank the problem part and leave it be for the moment above your left hand...

And I would now like your unconscious mind to go searching within yourself for the part of you that has the solution... the part of you that has exactly what this part needs to **easily sleep all night** now...

And I would like your unconscious mind to bring this part out and float it above your right hand...

/

Notice what this part may look like... perhaps it has a sound... or perhaps it has a feeling... or maybe even all three... however **this part manifests to you** now... become aware of it for a moment...

//

We shall refer to this part as the solution part... I would like you to now ask this solution part for insight as to what it will do for you... take a moment to interact with this part in this way Nowww...

//

I would like you to thank this part for its insight... and now I will begin to count up from 1 to 5 and with each number I count up, this solution part will become stronger...and stronger... and on the count of 5, this solution part will be 10 times stronger than the problem part...

So ready... 1... increasing the strength of the solution part... 2 more and more... 3 the solution part is already much stronger than the problem part... 4... and ... 5 the solution part is now 10 times stronger than the problem part...

Become aware of any changes that may have occurred during the strengthening process of the solution part...

//

And Now... in whatever way is appropriate for you... put the two parts together... merge the problem part with the solution part...

Since the solution is 10 times stronger than the problem... the solution part engulfs the problem part giving it exactly what it needs to **easily sleep all night** now...

As these two parts now merge... it forms a unified part which is now floating in the centre in between your hands...

/

Notice what this unified part may look like... perhaps it has a sound... or perhaps it has a feeling... or maybe even all three... however **this part manifests to you** now... become aware of it for a moment...

//

I would like you to thank this part for whatever it will do for you...

//

And Nowww... I would like you to reintegrate this part back within yourself... I will give you a moment of time to carry this out...

//

Very good... Nowww... I would like you to go back in time now to a memory or time when you were able to sleep very easily and deeply... perhaps this was sooner than you think... perhaps this was later... perhaps it was early childhood... whenever this was ... remember what this was like... and if you cannot find a memory... that is ok... simply imagine what it would be like to have a very restful night's sleep easily and deeply Nowww... I will give you a moment to do this...

///

Now that you are experiencing this memory... or creating it in your mind... see what you would see... perhaps being aware of what it would be like to wake up in the morning after a very sound... pleasant... restful... uninterrupted and deep sleep...

Your unconscious mind always knows how to induce deep sleep in you... you already know how to **fall asleep easily**... how to **sleep all night**... how to **sleep without interruption**... you have done this before very easily as a baby... now it is time to reconnect to something so easy... you've simply forgotten how easy it was... now it is time to remember... and you are now open and ready to remember... remember how to **fall asleep easily**... remember how to **sleep all night**... and how to **sleep without interruption**... that's right...

Every day you will begin to feel more relaxed... very calm... and relaxed... with a greater sense of self control... each and every day... as bedtime approaches... you will feel more and more pleasantly tired... each day... you will go to bed at the same time... each night at the same time... and as soon as you put your head on the pillow... you will begin to instantly relax...Nowww... exactly as you do...as you listen to this recording... your mind will become calm and relaxed... your whole body relaxes too... and as it does so more and more... you will begin to feel a pleasant feeling of heaviness in your body... as if... it is beginning to feel like lead... heavy as lead... as if it is very comfortably sinking down... deeper and deeper... into the mattress... and as it does so.. you will feel drowsier and drowsier... more and more drowsy... and presently... you may even find... that you try to stay awake... and the harder you try to stay awake... the drowsier you become and you will feel drowsier and drowsier... your eyes will close... and you will fall into a natural... healthy sleep which will last throughout the night... until your usual time for getting up in the morning... if for any reason you should wake up in the night... you will simply fix your gaze on the ceiling... and as you do so your eyelids... will feel so heavy and tired... heavy and tired... wanting to close... more and more... and a pleasant feeling of relaxation and drowsiness will once again flow through you… and you may find that you try to stay awake… and the harder you try to stay awake the drowsier you become and you will feel drowsier and drowsier and then… within a very short time your eyes will close… and you will fall into a natural sleep again… which will last until your usual time for getting up in the morning… that's right allow your unconscious mind to receive these suggestions and communicate this to all parts of you…

Your unconscious mind always knows how to induce deep sleep in you… you already know how to **fall asleep easily**… how to **sleep all night**… how to **sleep without interruption**… you have done this before very easily as a baby… now it is time to reconnect to something so easy… you've simply forgotten how easy it was… now it is time to remember… and you are now open and ready to remember… remember how to **fall asleep easily**… remember how to **sleep all night**… and how to **sleep without interruption**… that's right…

As the days go by... these suggestions will begin to take effect within you... and begin to rebalance the sleep rhythm in your body and mind... putting them in sync... allowing your mind and body to fall asleep simultaneously... as soon as your head touches the pillow every night... if your mind is very active in bed... as soon as you lie down in bed... your mind will begin to relax... as each thought floats away ...flows away like a boat in the sea... fading away... allowing your mind to relax... and Nowww there would be absolutely nothing for you to do right now... because regardless of what position you are lying down in... your body naturally adjusts itself to a comfortable position where your body can remain... allowing your mind and body both to **drift away ...drift away into a deep and healthy slumber**... and a sound... pleasant sleep... with no interruptions... a refreshing... healing... rejuvenating and healthy sleep... until your usual time for getting up in the morning...

Sleep easily... and sleep well... as you fall asleep pleasantly...so you will begin to have pleasant dreams... empowering dreams... that will aid you in sleep... that will aid you in the tasks of the next day and that will empower you to achieve your goals...

/

And I will give you just a moment of time which is all the time you need to just relax... and this will also assist all my suggestions to **sink deep** into your unconscious mind...

///

And... Nowww...I would like to thank your unconscious mind for its cooperation... and before I awaken you... I want you to know that... as each day goes by you are going to become a little more mentally calm... a little more clear in your mind... each and every day... which means that you will see things more clearly... think more clearly... so that no-one and nothing will ever be able to affect you or upset you in quite the same way.. your mind becomes clearer and clearer... crystal clear... allowing you to feel physically calm and relaxed too... not only in your body but you will also feel more emotionally calm and more relaxed about yourself... and about the world around you...

And you can enjoy these feelings of wellbeing each and every day no matter what you're doing, where you are or who you're with and you will find that you are going to feel fitter and stronger in every way... feeling more energetic... feeling more alert... enjoying a greater and greater sense of positive energy.... Feeling motivated and encouraged, positive and optimistic... each and every day...
You are safe... in the knowledge that your unconscious mind is always looking out for you...

As every day you are going to experience a greater feeling of well-being, mental as well as physical well-being... a greater feeling of safety and security too than you have felt in a long ...long time... allowing you to live your life in a way that is so much more satisfying...satisfying for you...

/

And... Nowww... I will begin to count up from 1 to 10 and with each number, I count up you will become 10 percent more awake, by the count of 8 your eyes will open, and by the count of 10 you will be wide awake and fully alert... and all natural and normal sensations will return to your limbs... and you will wake up feeling, rested, rejuvenated, relaxed, happy, and wonderful, ready for the rest of the day... ready to achieve your ideal weight and your dream body...

So...1...2...3 Drifting towards wakefulness...4...5...6 waking up more and more...7...8...open your eyes... 9... and 10... Wide awake, wide awake...fully wide awake...

Thank you for listening to this powerful hypnosis audio, please remember that the results will continue to increase long after the session has finished. The results get profoundly deeper each time you listen to this recording.

Session 2: Hypnosis Script - Body Anxiety & Overthinking

Overview: This session will focus on overcoming body anxiety and putting an end to overthinking.

Time: 60-minutes

[Reader Notes]

- The rhythm and pace are important therefore please read the following script at a steady pace, ensuring to take your time to guide the listener with your voice.
- Allow long comfortable pauses in between passages that you are happy with, and follow the key set out below to allow longer pauses.

- Embedded commands: Embedded commands will be written in bold, the reader must read the bold phrases at a slightly faster pace than the rest of the script. Eg: "See how easy it is to **Just Relax** Nowww", See how easy it is should be ready normally while "just relax" should be read slightly faster returning back to the normal pace when reading "Nowww".
- Nowww: The word "Nowww" should be emphasized and said on an out-breath as if sighing.

[Pause Key]

... Very short pause: Reader pauses for 2 seconds

/ Short pause: Reader pauses for 10 seconds

// Medium pause: Reader pauses for 20 seconds

/// Long pause: Reader pauses for 30 seconds

[Script Begins]

Welcome to the second session in the Weight-loss and Deep Sleep audiobook! A Hypnosis/Guided Meditation series.

This powerful hypnosis audio will focus on overcoming body anxiety and putting an end to patterns of overthinking.

Begin by finding a comfortable place where you can be alone for just a little while...
You can either sit down comfortably or lie down, please make sure your arms are by your sides and are uncrossed throughout the session.

Now you are in position, find a spot in front of you in the distance and simply gaze at this spot... and as you gaze at this spot notice as you breathe, each breath is relaxing you more and more...

Noticing that as you now stare at this spot your eyelids feel heavy and the more you stare the heavier your eyelids are becoming...

heavier and heavier. ...You may notice that you begin to blink more and more with each breath in... and each breath out... and I wonder how soon it will be before your eyes will close?... That's right just let your eyes close... let them close as you now bring your attention to your breath... And as you take a deep relaxing breath in through your nose... notice yourself going 3 times deeper with that breath out. That's right. Let go.

You may notice sounds around you, perhaps any sounds inside the room, or perhaps if you listen carefully you may hear sounds outside the room. All these sounds are unimportant, in fact in a strange and contradictory manner all these sounds will guide you deeper and deeper, making you feel better and better as the only sound of importance right now is the sound of my words and you can allow my words to pour relaxation throughout your mind... throughout your body... and throughout your awareness... that's right you're doing really well...

And... Nowww... I would like you to imagine that you are standing on a long empty road... notice what you may see... perhaps all the different shapes and shades of colours... noticing what time of day it is... becoming aware of the temperature of the air as it touches your skin... perhaps noticing the sounds around you... and as you breathe in... breathing in all those fragrances...

Now in a moment, I would like you to begin walking down this road... the road to change the way you see yourself... and how you think others perceive you... and how you perceive your body...

As you walk down this road... I will begin to count down from 10 to 1 and with each descending number from 10 and 1 ... each descending number will guide you 10 times deeper into that wonderful hypnotic state of relaxation... that in any event will become deeper and deeper as we go on... so... get ready...

Start walking down this road... the road to change... Nowww...10... Going deeper and deeper...9... Feeling better and better...with each step you take down this road... 8 ... The deeper you go the better you feel... 7... The better you feel the deeper you go... with each step you walk down this road 6... drifting ever more deeper still... and 5... feeling a sense of safety and security and 4... feeling a sense of optimism taking over you and you become open to letting go... 3 ... feeling free... 2... you are almost there... and...1... well done...

I would like you to know that every time I say the word deep... allow yourself to go 10 times deeper and deeper into that deep state of relaxation more and more...

And just know that the deeper you go the better you will feel and the better you will feel the deeper you will go... that's it...

Whenever I say the word fall, allow yourself to go 30 times deeper... so simply fall deep into that deep state of relaxation as you fall Nowww deep... deeper and deeper letting go... into that state of peace... into that state of calm soothing relaxation... pouring relaxation throughout your mind... throughout your body... and throughout your awareness... as you... fall deep Nowww...

And Nowww... as you reach the end of this road you see a grassy hill...and hear the sound of flowing water... as you follow the sound of the flowing water you see a grassy staircase leading down to a very magical looking riverbank...

The staircase contains 10 steps going down... approach this staircase and in a moment I will begin to countdown from 10 to 1 and with each descending number from 10 and 1 ... each descending number will guide you 20 times deeper into that wonderful hypnotic state of relaxation... that in any event will become even deeper and deeper as we go on... as you let go now...

Start walking down these stairs... these stairs leading down to the magical riverbank of change... Nowww...10... Going deeper and deeper...9... Feeling better and better...with each step you take down these stairs... 8 ... The deeper you go the better you feel... 7... The better you feel the deeper you go... with each step you walk down these stairs... 6... drifting ever more deeper still... moving closer and closer to the riverbank and 5... feeling a sense of safety and security and 4... feeling a sense of optimism taking over you and you become open to change and transformation... 3 ... feeling free... 2... you are almost there... and...1... you are doing really well...

Notice that you now stand before a very magical looking riverbank... the riverbank of change... the water of this very special riverbank has the ability to remove any worries... beliefs... labels... and anxieties related to how you feel about yourself... and how you feel about your body... the purifying water can remove all those worries about how you think other people may perceive you... notice that the water is clean and clear... smooth flowing.. beautiful... not a single rough edge or rock... Notice what you may see here by this river bank... perhaps all the different shapes and shades of colours... perhaps any vegetation... becoming aware of the temperature of the air as it touches your skin... perhaps noticing the sounds around you... and as you breathe in... breathing in all those fragrances... around this riverbank... make this experience vivid and real for you...

Now move closer up to the water... and take a look at your reflection... in the water... and as you look at your reflection... begin to notice that all your insecurities are beginning to manifest itself in the reflection... all those worries... anxieties about yourself... about your body... and now notice that as you put your hands into the water... the magical river begins to pull out from you... ever so gently and pleasantly all those insecurities... being pulled out of you... all those worries.. all those anxieties about the way you look... about the way your body looks... and all those negative beliefs and labels about how other people perceive you... allow the river to pull them out and... watch them flow down the river... away from you... all your worries... anxieties... and negative beliefs about your appearance now...

flowing away from you...in the river... the magical water... purifying them... allow this to take place for a moment now...

//

Nowww... that is done... imagine that all that is left of the insecurities... even those that may be too subtle for you to be aware of... your unconscious mind knows what they are.. simply allow these insecurities to drip down and out of your hands into the water... with each number I count down from 5 to 1... allow the last few insecurities that are left to trickle down your arms and right out of your palms and fingertips into the magical riverbank to flow right away from you Nowww... 5... feel those insecurities being accumulated and being pushed down from your shoulders... 4 ... you can let go of that heavy load now.... That you can feel lighter... allow it to flow down your arms...3... insecurities flowing down your elbows... 2... collecting in your palms ... the last few insecurities collecting in your palms... and... 1... allow them to drip right off your palms and into the water... flowing away from you... flick your hands into the water removing the last little drops... you are now... free... free from those burdens...

And Nowww... that all your worries... all your anxieties... and negative beliefs about your appearance and your body have now been pulled gently out of you and floated far away from you down the river...

Notice that there is a bridge nearby... that takes you to the other side of the river, approach this bridge and crossover to the other side... and notice that as you cross this bridge over the river... you are beginning to feel more and more optimistic about yourself... and when you cross to the other side... you notice there is a lake... this lake is still... it is so clear and steady... you can see the sky reflected off the surface of the still water... this water is like your mind... your thoughts... there are no ripples in the water... as you have been cleansed of all your anxieties and worries related to your body and how you and other people perceive your body...

Your mind can be crystal clear like this water... allow yourself to feel more and more confident about yourself... about the world around you and how other people perceive you... beauty... confidence and calmness lies within you... and you can begin to tap into it now... with each passing moment...

Similar to the riverbank this still water is also magical... a sip from this lake can produce a sense of confidence within yourself... connecting you to the eternal beauty that lies within you...

So... take a sip of the water from this still lake...and feel confidence flow through you... confidence about who you are... confidence about your body... confidence that you can achieve all your goals... you begin to feel more and more beautiful... and you know that when you feel beautiful inside... the world outside responds accordingly... so you know now consciously that as you tap into your inner confidence and inner beauty the world around you will see the confidence and beauty that you are … that can flow out through you…

And soon I will begin to count up from 1 to 10 and with each number I count up these feelings of confidence and beauty will begin to increase more and more and on the count of 10, these feelings of confidence and beauty will be 10 times stronger… 10 times stronger than it has ever been before…

So ready… 1… feel those feelings of confidence increase more and more… with each number I count up… 2… beauty… inner beauty increases more and more… feel beautiful… 3… these feelings of confidence and beauty are now 3 times stronger… becoming stronger and stronger… 4 filling you from the top of your head to the tips of your toes Nowww… 5 beginning to smile as you tap into your inner beauty and confidence… 6… rushing through you… feel the optimism… feel the glow… emanating through you… 7… these feelings becoming 7 times stronger than they have ever been before… 8 becoming excited… very excited to go out there and allow your confidence and inner beauty to shine forth and illuminate your life... 9... feel it growing more and more throughout your mind... throughout your body... and throughout your awareness... that's right... and... 10... feelings of confidence and beauty now 10 times stronger... 10 times stronger than it has ever been before... feel yourself light up... like the sun shining anew... lighting up the path to inner change and inner transformation...

And I will give you just a moment of time which is all the time you need to just relax... and this will also assist all my suggestions to sink deep into your unconscious mind...

///

And... Nowww...I would like to thank your unconscious mind for its cooperation... and before I awaken you... I want you to know that... as each day goes by you are going to become a little more mentally calm... a little more clear in your mind... each and every day... which means that you will see things more clearly... think more clearly... so that no-one and nothing will ever be able to affect you or upset you in quite the same way.. your mind becomes clearer and clearer... crystal clear... allowing you to feel physically calm and relaxed too... not only in your body but you will also feel more emotionally calm and more relaxed about yourself... and about the world around you...

Every day...you will feel a positive sense of strength... your mind clearer and calmer... tranquil... serene and focused and as the days...weeks ...and months go by and you feel ever more calm and relaxed in your mind and body...you will find that you think more clearly... concentrate more effectively... giving your whole undivided attention to whatever you are doing... and consequently, you will be able to see things in their truest perspective... and you become emotionally calmer... every day you remain more and more relaxed physically, emotionally, and mentally...coping appropriately with each and every situation you handle in your daily life...

And you can enjoy these feelings of wellbeing each and every day no matter what you're doing, where you are or who you're with and you will find that you are going to feel fitter and stronger in every way... feeling more energetic... feeling more alert... enjoying a greater and greater sense of positive energy.... Feeling motivated and encouraged, positive and optimistic... each and every day...

You are safe... in the knowledge that your unconscious mind is always looking out for you...

As every day you are going to experience a greater feeling of well-being, mental as well as physical well-being... a greater feeling of safety and security too than you have felt in a long ...long time... allowing you to live your life in a way that is so much more satisfying...satisfying for you...

/

And... Nowww... I will begin to count up from 1 to 10 and with each number, I count up you will become 10 per cent more awake by the count of 8 your eyes will open, and by the count of 10 you will be wide awake and fully alert... and all natural and normal sensations will return to your limbs... and you will wake up feeling, rested, rejuvenated, relaxed, happy, and wonderful, ready for the rest of the day... ready to achieve your ideal weight and your dream body...

So...1...2...3 Drifting towards wakefulness...4...5...6 waking up more and more...7...8...open your eyes... 9... and 10... Wide awake, wide awake...fully wide awake...

Thank you for listening to this powerful hypnosis audio, please remember that the results will continue to increase long after the session has finished. The results get profoundly deeper each time you listen to this recording.

Session 3: Hypnosis Script – Fat Burn & Exercise

Overview: This session will focus on direct suggestions for fat burning and motivation for exercising daily.

Time: 60-minutes

[Reader Notes]

- The rhythm and pace are important therefore please read the following script at a steady pace, ensuring to take your time to guide the listener with your voice.
- Allow long comfortable pauses in between passages that you are happy with, and follow the key set out below to allow longer pauses.
- Embedded commands: Embedded commands will be written in **bold**, the

reader must read the bold phrases at a slightly faster pace than the rest of the script. Eg: "See how easy it is to **Just Relax** Nowww", See how easy it is should be ready normally while "just relax" should be read slightly faster returning back to the normal pace when reading "Nowww".

- Nowww: The word "Nowww" should be emphasized and said on an out-breath as if sighing.

[Pause Key]

… Very short pause: Reader pauses for 2 seconds

/ Short pause: Reader pauses for 10 seconds

// Medium pause: Reader pauses for 20 seconds

/// Long pause: Reader pauses for 30 seconds

_____

[Script Begins]

Welcome to the third session in the Weight-loss and Deep Sleep audiobook! A Hypnosis/Guided Meditation series.

This powerful hypnosis audio will focus on suggestions for increased fat burning and motivation for exercising daily.

Begin by finding a comfortable place where you can be alone for just a little while...
You can either sit down comfortably or lie down, please make sure your arms are by your sides and are uncrossed throughout the session.

Now you are in position, bring your awareness to your eyelids and imagine that your eyelids are becoming heavy and tired... heavy and tired... and I wonder how soon it would be before they close... that's right... allow your eyes to close... and now... I would like you to begin tensing the muscles in your face more and more...and as you tense your muscles in your face...hold...and relax those muscles ...allow those muscles to go loose and limp drifting deeper and deeper... as you Nowww...

bring your awareness to your neck and begin to tense the muscles in your neck more and more... and Nowww... relax the muscles in your neck... allow them to go loose and limp... loose and limp relaxed... going deeper and deeper...

Guide your awareness now to the muscles of your shoulders, arms, hands, and fingers... tense those muscles more and more... hold the tension... and... relax... allow your shoulders... arms... hands and fingers to now relax... allow them to go loose and limp... loose and limp relaxed...

Nowww... allow your attention to move down to your chest...tensing the muscles in your chest more and more...hold the tension and...relax... allow the muscles of your chest to go loose and limp... loose and limp relaxed...going deeper and deeper Nowww... well done...

Begin to now tense the muscles in your stomach and abdomen... tensing those muscles... hold the tension... and... relax...allow the muscles of the stomach to go loose and limp...loose and limp relaxed...

Moving **down** to the muscles of your hips and buttocks... tense the muscles of your hips and buttocks more and more... hold the tension... and... relax... allow the muscles of your hips and buttocks to relax... and go loose and limp... loose and limp relaxed... going deeper and deeper and you relax...

And Nowww... the muscles of your thighs... tensing them more and more... hold the tension... and... relax... allow the muscles of your thighs to go loose and limp... loose and limp relaxed... going deeper and deeper...

Allow your attention to **go down** into your calves...allow the muscles of your calves to tense more and more... and hold this tension... and... now relax... allow the muscles of your calves to go loose and limp relaxed more and more...

And finally, **move down** to your feet... tensing the muscles in your feet... hold the tension...

and relax... allow the muscles in your feet to go loose and limp... loose and limp relaxed... going deeper and deeper...Nowww... you're doing really well...

Begin now to tense all the muscles in your body to the best of your ability from the top of your head to the tips of your toes...tense all your muscles... hold this tension... keep holding....and... relax... **let go** Nowww... allowing yourself to **sink deep** into this relaxation... **sink deep** into this state of peace...

That's right... relaxing more and more...continue to go deeper and deeper... with every word that I say... and soon you may begin to find that every sound... guides you deeper... every thought... guides you deeper... every breath in... and every breath out... guides you deeper and deeper... and even... every heartbeat guides you deeper and deeper still... so simply **let go** now... let go Nowww...
So... I would like you to imagine that you are standing on top of a spiral staircase that is going down... the staircase has 10 steps...

imagine yourself there... on top of that spiral staircase... and in a moment I will begin to count down from 10 to 1 and with each descending number from 10 and 1 I would like you to start walking down these stairs... to my count... and notice how with each descending number I count down from 10 to 1 you are going 10 times deeper than you have ever been before...

So ready... 10... Going deeper and deeper...9... Feeling better and better...with each step you take down these stairs... 8 ... The deeper you go the better you feel... 7... The better you feel the deeper you go... with each step you walk down these stairs... 6... drifting ever more deeper still... moving closer and closer to the bottom of the stairs... and 5... feeling a sense of safety and security and 4... feeling a sense of optimism taking over you and you become open to change and transformation... 3 ... feeling free... 2... you are almost there... and...1... you are doing really well...

Very good... Nowww imagine a bright light shining down from above melting away all of the excess fat on your body... imagine it flowing down off you... it will feel pleasant and wonderful... as you become lighter and lighter... this will remind your unconscious mind why you are here... and soon I will begin to countdown from 10 to 1 and with each number I count down... I would like you to notice yourself going even deeper and deeper and the excess weight begins to trickle down your body reaching the ground, leaving that lighter, healthier slimmer version of yourself... that was always there within... so... ready... 10... allow that excess fat... that excess weight to begin melting off as you go deeper and deeper still... 9... that's it more and more... going deeper and deeper... as that light cleanses you and heals whatever is underneath that excess fat as it melts off... 8... drifting ever more deeper still with every word that I say...7 ... imagining the excess fat reaching the ground as you go even deeper and deeper... 6... more and more deeper still with each passing moment that's right... 5...letting go... letting go of any resistance that may develop... as you go deeper and deeper... 4... letting go of any deep-rooted limiting beliefs that are preventing change... 3... feeling the freedom as you begin to feel lighter and lighter as all that excess weight begins to melt off you... 2...almost done... all of that weight is almost completely melted off you...and.... Nowww... 1... well done... all that excess weight has now melted off you as you are now free ... free from that excess weight... free from limiting beliefs and free from any resistances... very good... continue to go deeper and deeper ... more and more... solidify this message within your unconscious mind ... pave the way to inner transformation... to reach your weight goals and melt away that excess fat to reveal the healthier... slimmer... thinner version of yourself that was always there... so... Nowww... that we have set the stage... let us begin...

You are open and ready to **begin exercising** now... every day you will feel a sense of excitement to **start exercising** daily... imagine going back in time... back in time to a memory where you were really excited to do something... or go somewhere... perhaps to carry out a specific task... I will give you a moment of time to return back to this memory...

//

See what you were seeing... perhaps noticing the sounds around you... becoming aware of whether you were indoors or outdoors... alone or with someone... becoming aware of what it was you were excited to be doing... notice how it feels to **be excited**... to look forward to doing something... feel those sensations rush through your body....

And Nowww... I would like you to imagine a dial... very similar to a dial you would find on a radio which can be used to increase or decrease the volume... Imagine this dial...and it's currently set on 1...and it goes up to 10... in a moment I will begin counting up from 1 to 10 and with each number I count up... I would like you to turn up this dial notch by notch to my count... and notice that as you begin to turn up this dial to my count... each number I count up will cause those feelings of excitement to become stronger and stronger... so ready... grab hold of that dial... imagine it between your fingertips... turn up those feelings of excitement... Nowww... 1...2... feel those feelings of excitement increase more and more...3...turning up those feelings... 4... allow those feelings of excitement to grow... 5... filling your entire body as it increases... 6... filling you from the tips of your toes up to the top of your head...7... that's right... allow those feelings to grow... 8...feeling excited more and more...9... those feelings are almost at its peak... and... 10... allow the excitement to burst through you...

As soon as you wake up every morning and think about exercising all these feelings of excitement will return to you instantly and easily and you'll be filled with an immense urge to exercise...

It doesn't matter where you are... as soon as you wake up every morning and think about exercising all these feelings of excitement will return to you instantly and easily and you'll be filled with an immense urge to exercise...

Exercising will become more and more enjoyable each time you think about it... and after every workout, you will be more excited for the next session of physical exercise... You feel an immense sense of motivation to **begin immediately** now....

You know that as soon as you **begin exercising** daily... all you need to do is **continue exercising daily**... and you will begin to come closer and closer to your desired weight... and you are filled with excitement to make this a reality for you... because as soon as you wake up every morning and think about exercising, all these feelings of excitement will return to you instantly and easily and you'll be filled with an immense urge to exercise...

Your unconscious mind will begin to help your body...burn that excess fat... quicker and quicker every time... after every workout, your unconscious mind... facilitates the internal processes of the body to begin burning your excess fat at a quicker pace... and to ensure this process takes place at its optimum level you **exercise daily**... and **it is easy to exercise daily** Nowww... because you now know that as soon as you wake up every morning... and think about exercising all these feelings of excitement will return to you instantly and easily... and you'll be filled with an immense urge to exercise...

And Nowww... I would like your unconscious mind... the part of you that is responsible for motivation... that part of you that is responsible for excitement and the part of you which will ensure that as soon as you wake up every morning... and think about exercising, all these feelings of excitement will return to you instantly and easily... and you'll be filled with an immense urge to exercise... I would like your unconscious mind to relay this message to every part of you... to all of your bones... your ligaments... your muscles... all your cells... and all aspects of yourself, that **you are someone who exercises daily** Nowww...
You are someone who enjoys exercising now... and looks forward to a good session of exercise every single day... you do not feel quite right if you skip a session... you must exercise daily and feel the urge to exercise every single day...because... as soon as you wake up every morning and think about exercising all these feelings of excitement will return to you instantly and easily and you'll be filled with an immense urge to exercise... very good... you are doing really well...

And I will give you just a moment of time which is all the time you need to just relax... and this will also assist all my suggestions to **sink deep** into your unconscious mind...

///

And... Nowww...I would like to thank your unconscious mind for its cooperation... and before I awaken you... I want you to know that... as each day goes by you are going to become a little more mentally calm... a little more clear in your mind... each and every day... which means that you will see things more clearly... think more clearly... so that no-one and nothing will ever be able to affect you or upset you in quite the same way.. your mind becomes clearer and clearer... crystal clear... allowing you to feel physically calm and relaxed too... not only in your body but you will also feel more emotionally calm and more relaxed about yourself... and about the world around you...

And you can enjoy these feelings of well-being each and every day no matter what you're doing, where you are or who you're with and you will find that you are going to feel fitter and stronger in every way... feeling more energetic... feeling more alert... enjoying a greater and greater sense of positive energy.... Feeling motivated and encouraged, positive and optimistic... each and every day... You are safe... in the knowledge that your unconscious mind is always looking out for you...

Every day...you will feel a positive sense of strength... your mind clearer and calmer... tranquil... serene and focused and as the days...weeks ...and months go by and you feel ever more calm and relaxed in your mind and body...you will find that you think more clearly... concentrate more effectively... giving your whole undivided attention to whatever you are doing... and consequently, you will be able to see things in their truest perspective... and you become emotionally calmer... every day you remain more and more relaxed physically, emotionally, and mentally...coping appropriately with each and every situation you handle in your daily life...

As every day you are going to experience a greater feeling of well-being, mental as well as physical well-being... a greater feeling of safety and security too than you have felt in a long ...long time... allowing you to live your life in a way that is so much more satisfying...satisfying for you...

/

And... Nowww... I will begin to count up from 1 to 10 and with each number, I count up you will become 10 percent more awake by the count of 8 your eyes will open, and by the count of 10 you will be wide awake and fully alert... and all natural and normal sensations will return to your limbs... and you will wake up feeling, rested, rejuvenated, relaxed, happy, and wonderful, ready for the rest of the day... ready to achieve your ideal weight and your dream body...

So…1…2…3 Drifting towards wakefulness…4…5…6 waking up more and more…7…8…open your eyes… 9… and 10… Wide awake, wide awake…fully wide awake…

Thank you for listening to this powerful hypnosis audio, please remember that the results will continue to increase long after the session has finished. The results get profoundly deeper each time you listen to this recording.

Session 4: Hypnosis Script – Self-love & Integration

Overview: This session will focus on reconnecting the listener to self-love by using parts dissociation therapy and sealing off the sessions with self-integration work.

Time: 60-minutes

[Reader Notes]

- The rhythm and pace are important therefore please read the following script at a steady pace, ensuring to take your time to guide the listener with your voice.
- Allow long comfortable pauses in between passages that you are happy with, and follow the key set out below to allow longer pauses.

- Embedded commands: Embedded commands will be written in **bold**, the reader must read the bold phrases at a slightly faster pace than the rest of the script. Eg: "See how easy it is to **Just Relax** Nowww", See how easy it is should be ready normally while "just relax" should be read slightly faster returning back to the normal pace when reading "Nowww".
- Nowww: The word "Nowww" should be emphasized and said on an out-breath as if sighing.

[Pause Key]

… Very short pause: Reader pauses for 2 seconds

/ Short pause: Reader pauses for 10 seconds

// Medium pause: Reader pauses for 20 seconds

/// Long pause: Reader pauses for 30 seconds

[Script Begins]

Welcome to the fourth session in the Weight-loss and Deep Sleep audiobook! A Hypnosis/Guided Meditation series.

This powerful hypnosis audio will focus on reconnecting you to self-love and reinforcing the work we have done in the previous sessions.

Begin by finding a comfortable place where you can be alone for just a little while...
You can either sit down comfortably or lie down, please make sure your arms are by your sides and are uncrossed throughout the session.

Now you are in position, take a deep breath in through your nose... and let it out... Nowww... relax... and simply... allow your eyes to close... that's right... returning back... returning back into that state of peace... into that state of calm soothing relaxation... where you can **let go** more and more... drifting deeper and deeper with every word that I say...and soon you may begin to find that every sound... guides you deeper... every thought... guides you deeper... every breath in... and every breath out... guides you deeper and deeper... and even... every heartbeat guides you deeper and deeper still... so simply **let go** now... let go Nowww...

So... I would like you to imagine that you are standing on top of a hill with a long path that is going down... imagine yourself there... on top of that hill... and in a moment I will begin to count down from 10 to 1 and with each descending number from 10 to 1 I would like you to start walking down this path... to my count... and notice how with each descending number I count down from 10 to 1 you are going 10 times deeper than you have ever been before...

So ready... 10... Going deeper and deeper...9... Feeling better and better...with each step you take down this hill ... 8 ... The deeper you go the better you feel... 7... The better you feel the deeper you go... with each step you walk down this path... 6... drifting ever more deeper still... moving closer and closer to the bottom of the hill... and 5... feeling a sense of safety and security and 4... feeling a sense of optimism taking over you and you become open to change and transformation... 3 ... feeling free... 2... you are almost there... and...1...

...you're doing very well.. remain deeply relaxed and imagine that now there is a very magical looking door that appears in the field below...the door leads to a very special room...

It is a beautifully decorated room of learning... a room of learning which will have a large whiteboard on the wall...

So open that door... and walk into this room... see what you would see... perhaps noticing if there are any items in this room... noticing the whiteboard... perhaps being aware of any sounds that would be present here...

I want you Nowww... to go over to the whiteboard... quite close by I would like you to find a white board marker pen and an eraser... I want you Nowww... to stand in front of the whiteboard... I want you to take the marker pen and write the number 5 at the top of the board... as you begin to draw... notice how you form the number 5... see the number 5 on the whiteboard ... now when you can see the 5 ... I want you to take the eraser and wipe it away... wipe away the number 5... breathe and relax... Very Good...

Nowww... write on the board with the marker... the words **deep sleep**... and as you write these words clearly... allow yourself to go 20 times deeper and deeper... Nowww...

Wipe these words clean off the board using the eraser and allow your mind to clear... as you now begin to write the number 4 on the board... until you can see it clearly... and Nowww... erase the number 4... wipe it away... breathe and relax...

Nowww... write on the board with the marker... the words **let go**... and as you write these words clearly... allow yourself to go 20 times deeper and deeper... Nowww...
Wipe these words clean off the board using the eraser and allow your mind to clear... as

you now begin to write the number 3 on the board... until you can see it clearly... and Nowww... erase the number 3... wipe it away... breathe and relax...

Nowww... write on the board with the marker... the words **Drifting deeper**... and as you write these words clearly... allow yourself to go 20 times deeper and deeper... Nowww...

Wipe these words clean off the board using the eraser and allow your mind to clear... as you now begin to write the number 2 on the board... until you can see it clearly... and Nowww... erase the number 2... wipe it away... breathe and relax... That's right...

Nowww... write on the board with the marker... the words **deeply relaxed**... and as you write these words clearly... allow yourself to go 20 times deeper and deeper... Nowww...

Wipe these words clean off the board using the eraser and allow your mind to clear... as you now begin to write the number 1 on the board... until you can see it clearly... and

Nowww... erase the number 1... wipe it away... breathe and relax... you are doing really well...

And... Now... Nowww... write on the board with the marker... the words **let go completely**... and as you write these words clearly... allow yourself to go 20 times deeper and deeper... Nowww...

However... this time when you wipe these words off... allow your mind to go blank... as you drift 30 times deeper and deeper... Nowww...

You are very... very deeply relaxed... allow yourself to relax deeper... and deeper still... listen carefully to the things that I tell you... and ask of you... because everything I say will happen... it will happen exactly as I describe... let your inner mind absorb my words and suggestions ... they will become part of your reality so that the positive effects will also be a reality for you... you will be able to talk and respond to me when asked and you will remain completely relaxed and in trance...

And... Nowww... I would like to speak with your unconscious mind about a matter of importance, important to you...

I would like you to know that if this session gets interrupted in any way that your unconscious mind will ensure that all parts of you will naturally be reintegrated within yourself...

/

I would like your unconscious mind... the part of you that has the answer to all problems... the part of you that has access to all parts of you... to go searching within yourself for the part of you that is lacking or blocking self-love...

And I would like your unconscious mind to bring this part out and float it above your left hand...

/

Notice what this part may look like... perhaps it has a sound... or perhaps it has a feeling... or maybe even all three... however **this part manifests to you** now... become aware of it for a moment...

//

We shall refer to this part as the problem part... I would like you to now ask this problem part for insight as to what it is really doing for you...why is it really here... take a moment to interact with this part in this way Nowww...

//

Nowww... let this part know... that whatever this part needs to **reconnect to self-love** now... there is another part of you that has exactly what this part needs to **reconnect to self-love** now...

//

Let this part know that you will now go searching for the part of you that has exactly what that parts need to **reconnect to self-love** ...

//

So Nowww... I would like you to thank the problem part and leave it be for the moment above your left hand...

And I would now like your unconscious mind to go searching within yourself for the part of you that has the solution... the part of you that has exactly what this part needs to **reconnect to self-love** now...

And I would like your unconscious mind to bring this part out and float it above your right hand...

/

Notice what this part may look like... perhaps it has a sound... or perhaps it has a feeling... or maybe even all three... however **this part manifests to you** now... become aware of it for a moment...

//

We shall refer to this part as the solution part... I would like you to now ask this solution part for insight as to what it will do for you... take a moment to interact with this part in this way Nowww...

//

I would like you to thank this part for its insight... and now I will begin to count up from 1 to 5 and with each number I count up, this solution part will become stronger...and stronger... and on the count of 5, this solution part will be 10 times stronger than the problem part...

So ready... 1... increasing the strength of the solution part... 2 more and more... 3 the solution part is already much stronger than the problem part... 4... and ... 5 the solution part is now 10 times stronger than the problem part...

Become aware of any changes that may have occurred during the strengthening process of the solution part...

//

And Now... in whatever way is appropriate for you... put the two parts together... merge the problem part with the solution part...

Since the solution is 10 times stronger than the problem... the solution part engulfs the problem part giving it exactly what it needs to **reconnect to self-love** now...

As these two parts now merge... it forms a third unified part which is now floating in the centre in between your hands...

/

Notice what this unified part may look like... perhaps it has a sound... or perhaps it has a feeling... or maybe even all three... however **this part manifests to you** now... become aware of it for a moment...

//

I would like you to thank this part for whatever it will do for you...

//

And Nowww... I would like you to reintegrate this part back within yourself... I will give you a moment of time to carry this out...

//

Very good... Nowww... We all have skin that very clearly separates that which is inside of us... from that which is outside of us... just like the skin on our body, it separates our blood vessels, internal organs, and bones from that which is outside of us...

Similarly, our mind also has a skin that separates that which is inside of us from that which is outside of us... like a boundary... for some people it may be as if they have a circle around them... some people may find it to be like being encased in a bubble...or a force field... or even a shell...

I wonder what your mental skin... your boundary would look like... I wonder whether it would have a particular sound... I wonder what size it would be... I wonder what it would be made out of... I will go silent for a little while... giving you a moment of time which is all the time you need to imagine what your boundary would be like...

//

Nowww... in whatever shape or form your boundary has manifested in... I would like you to imagine that there is a little door in your boundary which you can open and close to let things in and push things out...

You have complete control over what comes in and what goes out of your boundary...

/

And Nowww... I would like you to imagine that within your boundary are parts of yourself that are no longer serving you... that in fact are causing detriment to you... allow your unconscious mind to guide you... and you know intuitively what parts you need to push out of your boundary... I will give you a moment of time to locate these aspects...

/

Nowww... imagine opening the door to your boundary and pushing these detrimental parts out of your boundary, away from you... pushing these detrimental aspects that are no longer serving you right out of your boundary...

/

And Nowww... I would like you to imagine that outside of your boundary are parts of yourself that are in fact useful to you... parts of yourself that are beneficial to your well-being...

Allow your unconscious mind to guide you... and you intuitively know what these aspects are... I will give you a moment of time to locate these aspects...

/

And Nowww... in whatever way is appropriate for you I would like you to pull in these aspects of yourself... inside your boundary... pulling in all these useful... empowering aspects within your boundary...

/

Close the door to your boundary now... only you can open and close this door...
In a moment I will begin to count up from 1 to 10 and with each number I count up I would like your boundary to become stronger and stronger in every way... improving in every way... for your current needs... reinforcing... strengthening...

1... improving your boundary more and more... 2 becoming stronger... 3 becoming reinforced... 4... more and more ...5 go deeper and deeper as this process takes place... 6... 7... 8... improving your boundary... 9... it's almost complete... and... 10...

Become aware of your new and improved boundary... notice what it looks like... notice if it has a particular sound or feeling associated with it... notice what its size is... notice what it is made out of...

/

Whenever you need a sense of self-control and strength... you will naturally become aware of your boundary.. formulating around you... filling you with strength and self-control... this process will happen naturally and unconsciously... filling you with all the positive qualities provided by the positive aspects of yourself that you have pulled into your boundary...

/

Nowww... simply allow the boundary to fade away... knowing that it is always in place... providing you with these inner positive qualities...

And Nowww... I will give you just a moment of time, which is all the time you need, to just relax and enjoy this state, and this will also assist all my suggestions to **sink deep** into your unconscious mind...

///

And... Nowww...I would like to thank your unconscious mind for its cooperation...
Each and every day no matter what you're doing, where you are or who you're with and you will find that you are going to feel fitter and stronger in every way... feeling more energetic... feeling more alert... enjoying a greater and greater sense of positive energy....
Feeling motivated and encouraged, positive and optimistic... each and every day...

You are safe... in the knowledge that your unconscious mind is always looking out for you...

Every day...you will feel a positive sense of strength... your mind clearer and calmer... tranquil... serene and focused and as the days...weeks ...and months go by and you feel ever more calm and relaxed in your mind and body...you will find that you think more clearly... concentrate more effectively... giving your whole undivided attention to whatever you are doing...

As every day you are going to experience a greater feeling of well-being, mental as well as physical well-being... a greater feeling of safety and security too than you have felt in a long ...long time... allowing you to live your life in a way that is so much more satisfying...satisfying for you...

/

And... Nowww... I will begin to count up from 1 to 10 and with each number, I count up you will become 10 percent more awake by the count of 8 your eyes will open, and by the count of 10 you will be wide awake and fully alert... and all natural and normal sensations will return to your limbs... and you will wake up feeling, rested, rejuvenated, relaxed, happy, and wonderful, ready for the rest of the day... ready to achieve your ideal weight and your dream body...

So...1...2...3 Drifting towards wakefulness...4...5...6 waking up more and more...7...8...open your eyes... 9... and 10... Wide awake, wide awake...fully wide awake...

Thank you for listening to this powerful hypnosis audio, please remember that the results will continue to increase long after the session has finished. The results get profoundly deeper each time you listen to this recording.

Session 5: Guided Meditation - Overcoming Insomnia

Time: 30 mins

[Reader Notes]

- Read the following script at a steady pace, taking your time to guide the meditator/listener with your voice.
- Allow comfortable pauses that you are happy with, and follow the key set out below to allow longer pauses.

[Pause Key]

/ Short pause: The reader takes a long breath.
// Medium pause: The reader pauses for 30 seconds.
/// Long pause: The reader pauses for 2 minutes +

[Meditation Begins]

Welcome to this guided meditation for overcoming insomnia as you continue on your weight loss journey brought to you by _____.

Begin this guided meditation before you get into bed. Overcoming insomnia is a process, and research shows that you are more likely to enjoy quality rest and even sleep by beginning with a bedtime ritual.

/

You see, Insomnia is a sleep disorder that affects at least 50% of adults at least once in their lifetime. When we become overly stressed, anxious, fearful or even overly stimulated, it can prove difficult to enjoy good quality sleep. Sleep is a vital component of the weight loss journey, and so by listening to this guided meditation, you can begin to overcome insomnia and increase your weight loss as a result.

/

Standing next to your bed, take a few deep breaths.
Now is a good time to centre yourself in this moment.
Before you climb into bed, bring your awareness to the tiredness in the body right now.

/

Your mental checklist will pop up soon.
Allow your mind to scan the list.
Closed the window, check.

Front door locked, check.

Garden lights off, check.

Alarm set, check.

/

Allow any last-minute thoughts to pass.
What am I going to wear tomorrow?

Wonder if I'll get a seat on the train.

I must try and eat healthily tomorrow.

Like clouds in the sky, your thoughts may keep coming,
One after the other, morphing into new thoughts,
Creeping across the sky, slowly drifting away,
Until eventually, they pass in their usual monotonous way.

//

Dim the lights if you haven't already done so.
Make sure the temperature of the room is just right.

Scribble down any last-minute tasks or lingering ideas.

Close your laptop.

Silence your mobile phone.

Put any other screens away.

And snuggle down beneath the sheets.

Permitting yourself to relax

///

Allow your thoughts to turn to gratitude. What are you grateful for today?

A nice cup of coffee this morning.

A great conversation with your colleague at work.

A funny joke told by a friend.

A heartwarming story on Facebook.

Allow your gratitude to expand as you relax. Letting the feelings of gratitude and calm spread throughout your body.

///

Now that you have completed your bedtime ritual

You can relax and let go as you lie down,
Feel the body assume its usual resting position.
Allow the breath to cultivate relaxation in the body and mind.

/

As you breathe in, feel the lungs fill with air.
When you exhale, feel the body soften into your mattress.
Picture yourself falling deeper into the mattress as the body relaxes with each exhale.
Lie on your back with your arms relaxed by your sides.
Take a moment to get comfortable.
Slowly close your eyes, or focus on one spot on the floor or wall.
Invite your body and mind to begin to relax.

///

Our brains benefit from quality sleep, our bodies benefit from quality sleep, and those around us benefit when we enjoy a good night's sleep. Quality sleep helps with focus and attention; it helps with clarity and emotional intelligence. There is nothing that cannot be achieved following a good night's sleep.

[Quote]
"William Shakespeare once said, Let her sleep for when she wakes she will move mountains."

As you wind down now,
Everything is taken care of.

As you close your eyes,
Allow the muscles around the eyes to relax.

Allow your head to sink deeply into the pillow.
Let your arms and shoulders fall.

Allow the breath to soften your back.
Loosen the hips and pelvis.

And as you exhale, let your ankles, feet and knees relax.
Just relaxing deeper with every breath you take.

///

Allow any thoughts of worry or the passing day to just be present in your mind.
There is no need to push them away or stop them.
Take a nice relaxing deep breath in.
And as you exhale, drop your shoulders down, release your hands, fingers and jaw.
Close your eyes and drop your brow, now breathe.

///

As you breathe at your regular pace,
bring your full awareness to your thoughts.

Perhaps there are thoughts of worrying about your weight.
Maybe you are afraid that you won't lose the weight.
Perhaps you are concerned that you are not losing weight fast enough.
Whatever your thoughts are at this time,
There is no need to push or pull them in any direction.

There is no need to challenge your thoughts at all.
Just observe and identify any pressing ideas about your weight or anything else.

///

If your thoughts become overwhelming, simply take a breath.
Now return your full awareness to noticing the breath,
then allow your attention to drift to your thoughts once again.
Following any thoughts, seeing where your mind may wander,
take a few moments to notice your worries,
there is no need to judge them or alter them in any way,
just observe them.

//

When we begin to notice how much we worry,
when we worry, and why we worry,
we can begin to release our worries.

So, using the breath to guide you,
once again, follow your mind,
as it wanders towards your fears,
and just observe whatever you find there.

///

[Quote]
"Worrying is using your imagination to create something you don't want - Abraham Hicks."

The imagination is a powerful tool that can help us to create stories in our minds,
many of which are worries about the future.

When we become concerned about losing weight or a lack of weight loss, this can cause insomnia, anxiety and even depression.
Did you know that 5 - 10% of worries are problems that we can solve, and most of our fears never actually materialise; they are often just the result of our vivid imaginations?

//

Become aware of these worries or concerns about your weight, and remind yourself that many of these worries are simply imagined worries.

The good news is that now you can begin to release these worries and enjoy a good night's sleep; as you know, sleep is an essential component of weight loss.

So by releasing these figments of your imagination, you will begin to overcome insomnia and boost your weight loss journey.

///

Focus on your breathing, once again following your breath,
as it comes into your body and goes out of your body.
Imagine that with each breath in; you're breathing in drowsiness and relaxation,
and with each breath out, you're releasing racing thoughts and weight loss worries.

Now, return your awareness to your breathing.
And take a long deep breath in.

Enjoy breathing and filling the body and mind with fresh, rejuvenating air.
And now, I would like you to redirect your imagination as I take you on a journey.

///

Now I am going to take you on a guided visualisation journey.
One where all you have to do is listen to my voice and relax.
And as you join me on this journey, I will guide you into a state of rest.
Where even if you do not fall asleep,
your body will still get the rest it needs to accelerate your weight loss.

///

Continue breathing deeply another five times. Making sure to breathe out fully and completely.
As you make way for a fresh breath coming in each time.

///

The mind is just like the sun.
Each morning the mind awakens like the sun rising in the sky,
at night, the mind relaxes just as the sun sets on the horizon.
Imagine sitting outside in a comfortable chair, now
a little before sunset, and you're facing in the direction of the setting sun.
Notice if there are clouds in the sky,
Now begin to notice the colours you see in the sky.
As the sun is just starting to set, imagine seeing different shades of red in the sky.
As you begin to relax the mind, imagine seeing that red in the sky fade to a softer orange.
As the light slowly continues to fade in the sky, allow your mind to slow down, and begin to relax deeply.
Imagine your body becoming more comfortable as the colour fades in the sky.
And slowly, you start to see some pinks in between the soft orange colours.
Notice how gentle and calm your mind feels now.

As the sun continues to set,
you might see some soft purple hues in the sky.
Imagine your body becoming more and more comfortable,
letting any distractions fade just as the colours in the sky are fading.

//

Notice the sky becoming slightly darker,
Imagine your mind continuing to relax.
Notice that the sun is just about gone now,
as your mind surrenders to the comfort of rest.

///

Now, you can invite your body and mind
to continue to feel comfortable and relaxed,
even as your attention drifts elsewhere.
Clear any last thoughts as your mind slows down,
as you drift, just drifting into deep relaxation.

Your mind can continue to slow down,

as your body finds comfort in the soft cosy bed and just as the colours in the sunset have faded,
this meditation draws to a close.
Sweet dreams.

Session 6: Guided Meditation - Self Love & Weight Loss

Time: 30 mins

[Reader Notes]

- Read the following script at a steady pace, taking your time to guide the meditator/listener with your voice.
- Allow comfortable pauses that you are happy with, and follow the key set out below to allow longer pauses.

[Pause Key]

/ Short pause: The reader takes a long breath.
// Medium pause: The reader pauses for 30 seconds.
/// Long pause: The reader pauses for 2 minutes +

[Meditation Begins]

Welcome to this guided meditation for increasing self love and weight loss brought to you by _____.

Hello and welcome to this guided meditation, where you will experience a strong sense of self-love as you enter into relaxation. We all know how important rest and sleep are for weight loss, but how often do you consider the part that self-love and acceptance play in your weight loss journey?

One of the reasons that many people regain the weight they lose is due to a need for protection or a negative self-image. Some people simply do not believe they deserve to be slim and healthy, while others feel safer and more comfortable when they are heavier and more vulnerable when they are thinner.

So, although you may express a desire to lose weight, sometimes the subconscious beliefs you hold can cause you to hold onto it.

The following meditation will assist you in accepting your body in its natural slimmer healthier state, and help you to increase your inner strength and power.
So when you are ready and feel comfortable and supported, we can begin the meditation.

///

You are about to embark on a guided meditation journey, where I will guide you into a deep state of relaxation in which you will experience a calmness and meditative state of mind.

This time is for you and you alone, and all you have to do is relax and allow yourself to have this time and do whatever feels suitable for you as you relax.

And now, I would simply like you to focus on your breath.

Breathe in deeply

Exhale fully

Breathe in deeply

Exhale fully

Breathe in deeply

Exhale fully

//

You may notice some thoughts and self-talk in your mind; that's okay, allow them to pass by, and they will slow down as you concentrate on listening to the sounds in the background.

/

And now, as you breathe deeply, you will find that your mind gently begins to quiet.

Breath in deeply

Exhale fully

Breathing in the cool refreshing air

Exhaling any negative, warm, tense air

The more you listen, the more relaxed you feel.

Allow yourself to be in total peace with your surroundings.

Now, as you relax, calm your mind.

Breathe deeply

Exhale fully

Feel the incredible sense of deep relaxation wash over you, calming and soothing

And now I would like you to join me on a journey.

A journey deep into your imagination, are you ready?

/

And now you see yourself in a beautiful garden.
A private garden where you are the only one in the garden.
This garden is exotic. It has palm trees and birds singing in the trees.
As you begin to walk through the garden, you notice a light warm breeze and the sun starting to set.
It's calm and quiet apart from the sound of the birds singing.
The leaves bristle on the breeze, and in the distance, you hear the sound of water.

///

As you walk towards the sound, eventually you come to a clearing, and in the clearing, you notice a vast waterfall. It is, in fact, the most impressive waterfall you have ever seen.

///

And as you stand in front of the waterfall, you see a bench and decide to sit.

Listening to the sound of the waterfall is a new experience.
It is as if the intense rushing sound of the water as you sit up close is somehow penetrating your mind and your body.
Every cell reverberates with the pounding of the water as it hits the rocks beneath it. The smell is vibrant and fresh. The energy is powerful and breathtaking.

///

The wonder of being here with this waterfall affects every sense.
The sight, the sound, the sensation, the smell, it's all so beautiful and yet so intimidating.

///

This moment is the moment where you release all of your thoughts of judgement, self-doubt and loathing to the power of the waterfall.
Allow each of them to be emptied from your mind into the rushing intensity of the water.
Allow the waterfall to rush them away, pound

them on the rocks beneath it to dissolve them into nothingness. Let them go.

///

And now imagine the intensity of the pounding water pushing away the tension you feel in your body.
You are allowing the tension to be pummeled out of your body by the power of the waterfall. Let every part of your body be relieved of the stress or anxiety that has caused you to gain weight. Let your mind be cleansed of the self-critical words of hate and disgust.
Surrender it all to the power of the waterfall.
You are safe here. All is secure so that you can surrender. Remember this is your safe place, where nobody can enter; it's just you and the cleansing power of your waterfall.

///

Now notice how the longer you sit, the more your concerns and doubts about life are washed away. See how any doubts you had

about your ability to release weight are washed away.
Notice how any doubts you ever had about being slim and toned and healthy are rushed away in the avalanche of water.

///

Let go of all negative thoughts, release them into the waterfall, allowing you to make space for new, positive thoughts and beliefs, for unlimited beliefs that will serve you in your journey of weight loss. Replace the negative with positive as you allow any doubts about your healthy, fit body and future weight management to simply dissolve into the rigorous flow of the waterfall.

///

Now is the time to throw in any doubts about your ability to release excess fat through healthy eating and exercise and have them washed away.

Release any beliefs that it's hard to lose weight or tone and improve your physical body and allow them to be washed away.

Replace those thoughts with thoughts of confidence that you do lose weight now.

Throw into the waterfall any thoughts or beliefs of excess weight being protective or suitable for you and watch as they are rushed away by the relentless flow of the waterfall.

Replace these with great thoughts of how weight loss is improving your life and making everything better.

///

For the first time in a long time, tell yourself you are sure, you are confident that losing weight is a beautiful new experience for you.
Weight loss brings new and happy experiences.
Weight loss is the key to a safe and protected life.

Weight loss brings you much of the joy and happiness that you seek in life.
Weight loss is a positive change in your life.

///

I want you to know that you are good enough to let the weight go.
You are better without it.
You have the inner strength to protect yourself.
You are more vital when you are fitter.
You are truly capable of achieving all of your weight loss goals quickly.

///

I want you to know that you are powerful and beautiful.
You are strong and healthy.
You are sexy and divine.
You think and feel positive thoughts and feelings about your body right now.
You are sure and secure about your body without the extra weight.

You are confident that life is better without excess weight.

///

And as you look around this beautiful exotic paradise sat in front of this powerful waterfall, you wonder at the power of the water and the ability to wash away the negative and replace it with the positive.

Just before we bring this meditation to a close,
repeat these affirmations after me;

I love myself
I accept myself
I am worthy of self-love
I am worthy of a slim and toned body
I am worthy of a lean and healthy body
I am strong enough to protect myself
I love myself
I am proud of myself
I am doing a good job every day of my life
I am putting myself and my needs first every day

I love my weight loss journey
I am in love with myself and my body
I am a beautiful and powerful person
I have an unshakeable belief in my body
I am making the best healthy weight loss choices daily
I always attract only the most nutritious foods
I engage in only the most positive habits and activities
I love and appreciate every part of my body
I am proud of the way I look
I am full of health, strength, beauty and vitality

///

And again

I love myself
I accept myself
I am worthy of self-love
I am worthy of a slim and toned body
I am worthy of a lean and healthy body
I am strong enough to protect myself
I love myself
I am proud of myself
I am doing a good job every day of my life

I am putting myself and my needs first every day
I love my weight loss journey
I am in love with myself and my body
I am a beautiful and powerful person
I have an unshakeable belief in my body
I am making the best healthy weight loss choices daily
I always attract only the most nutritious foods
I engage in only the most positive habits and activities

I love and appreciate every part of my body
I am proud of the way I look
I am full of health, strength, beauty and vitality

///

And you know that you can return at any time to your safe place alone.
Whenever you notice those doubts or negative self-talk creeping back in, listen to this guided meditation again and surrender those thoughts to the waterfall.

This is your special secret safe, peaceful place where you can relax, just sit beside the waterfall where there is no judgement, no pressure, no stress, only peace, calm and the sounds and smells of this beautiful exotic hideaway.

///

Whenever you need to experience a positive moment where you can impress thoughts of well-being and goodness on your subconscious, you know you can return to the waterfall.
You understand that this is the place where you make your best decisions, develop your best beliefs, where you enjoy your thoughts of love, positivity and self-belief; you are reminded of your true beauty, and you feel your power.

///

Just like the power of the waterfall, you can give yourself the gift of being in the moment and having perfect inner peace, the place where you feel satisfied with your life because you know your life is the ideal journey for you and you know that everything is working together for your good.

///

And then, as the waterfall continues in the background, you begin to sense your thoughts slowly coming back, and you become aware of your breath once again, and you slowly rise to your feet.

As you walk back to the exit of the private garden, you continue to feel beautiful, powerful and confident, and as you return to the thoughts of the evening ahead, you feel healthy, strong and sure of your weight loss journey improving your life.

You can be sure that this is your rightful state, slim, toned and healthy.

As we near the end of this session, take a moment to reflect on what you have just experienced. Hopefully, you managed to follow my guidance throughout this meditation and practised releasing all of the negative thoughts and doubts that you held about weight loss.

/

Whatever you noticed from today's meditation, you can be proud of the fact that you are well on your way to losing weight and increasing your sense of self-love and acceptance.

/

When you're ready, take a long, slow breath in and as you exhale, open your eyes or lift your gaze, wiggle your fingers and toes, and gently come back to the room.

/

Remember, meditation is a practice, and just like any other skill, it requires effort and repetition.

Once this meditation is over, as you go about the rest of your day or evening, see if you can take brief moments to practice releasing any negative thoughts about weight loss or yourself.

Whenever you do manage to release these thoughts, practice replacing them with a positive life-affirming thought in its place.

Session 7: Guided Meditation - Deep Sleep For Rapid Weight Loss

Time: 60 mins

[Reader Notes]

- Read the following script at a steady pace, taking your time to guide the meditator/listener with your voice.
- Allow comfortable pauses that you are happy with, and follow the key set out below to allow longer pauses.

[Pause Key]

/ Short pause: The reader takes a long breath.
// Medium pause: The reader pauses for 30 seconds.
/// Long pause: The reader pauses for 2 minutes +

[Meditation Begins]

Welcome to this guided meditation for Deep Sleep and Rapid Weight Loss, brought to you by _____.

Welcome, dear friends….it is such a pleasure to have you join me on this deep sleep rapid weight loss guided meditation.

It is time to relax, unwind, and leave the day behind.

And as you get ready for a good night's rest, take a few deep breaths and just tell yourself that now is a good time to lay back, relax and take a mental vacation to the beach.

/

And as you make yourself comfortable, loosening any tight clothing, adjusting your position to one of comfort and support, it's time to drift off to your very own private Caribbean island where you will find a luxury beach hut waiting just for you.

///

So as we begin, set your intentions for deep relaxation - rapid weight loss overnight and a good night's sleep.

///

And as you ponder on the day that has just gone by or even the day ahead, allow your thoughts to slow and your mind to be at ease.

And as you look forward to a night of rest and repair for your body and your mind you can be optimistic about the good night's sleep that lies ahead.

//

And now, you are here with me, anticipating your journey into sleep. We can begin with some deep relaxation techniques to help you to release the tension and tightness that you may have developed throughout the day, these techniques will cause rapid weight loss.

///

So close your eyes or lower your gaze if this is more comfortable, allow your body to become limp as you allow the bed or couch beneath you to support your weight and begin with deep cleansing breaths.
Breathing in as deeply and fully as you can, filling the lungs and chest space on every inhale.

///

And as you exhale push the air out gradually, ensuring you empty the lungs in preparation for the next deep breath in.

And enjoy the relaxation that deep breathing provides, enjoy the sensation of breathing deeply and fully. Enjoy the experience of allowing your breath to relieve any tension in the muscles or any tightness in the limbs, all adding to your rapid weight loss.

And when you feel suitably relaxed you can allow your body to return to its natural pattern of breathing.

//

And as you lie here with your breath, this is a good time to see your personal speedboat in your imagination.

You may have sailed your own boat before or this may be your first time, just go ahead and create the image in your mind, the colour, the shape and the size.

///

And see yourself as a competent sailor, you have the ability and the know-how to sail your own boat, what a great way to relax and ease the body and the mind.

And now it's time to embark on your relaxing boat ride, sailing across the Caribbean sea in your very own small speedboat, to a secluded desert island, where you will be able to luxuriate in the privacy of a private beach hut without any interruption or disturbance.

///

And as you lay here, allow the music to guide you into deep relaxation. Let your thoughts dissolve into dreamy notions of the crystal blue seas that surround your green tropical island.

//

Let go of any tightness in the body that is holding onto the weight and gently breathe in the clean sea air, letting it cleanse and clear the cells of the body as you continue breathing out any tension or tightness.

/

And I'd like you to imagine now stepping into your speedboat and as you start the engine the gentle bubbling of the propeller in the water, gives you a sense of comfort and ease.

And as you take a hold of the rudder now you begin to guide your boat across the surface of the bluest clearest waters you have ever seen.

//

The sky above is light and airy with just a hint of blue, not a cloud to be seen just the occasional bird high up above as the ocean breeze caresses your body, keeping you cool and calm as you glide across the sea.

//

And as you begin to think about ways you can increase your weight loss through relaxation, start with one small area of your body where there is a little tension.

And just notice this area of tension at first. Perhaps acknowledging how it got there. Where it came from, and as you focus on this small spot of tightness, you can allow it to ease slightly, letting go of any excess weight, as you relax and repair the muscles, cells and limbs in the body.

///

And when you're ready to completely let go, take a deep breath in. And as you exhale drop the muscles and feel the full release.

//

And as you begin to slowly move through the water - check-in with yourself.
Noticing where you are tense,
holding or clenching in the body.

Check-in with the feet first,
noticing the ankles, and the toes.

Let them go.
Allow them to drop forward and wiggle the toes to make sure they are not gripping with tension.

///

And as you release the feet take a deep breath in if you need, to ensure you completely release them. Then take a look around at the open water.

The low waves gently lapping against the side of the boat are not too much or too little just enough to keep you moving gently across the sea.

///

And as you enjoy the beautiful turquoise waters, take another deep breath in and release the calves, perhaps clenching the muscles first for a count of 3 ...1...2...3...and then releasing and relaxing the legs completely as you exhale.

///

Feel how heavy your legs are becoming now as you release the tension that you were holding onto. Knowing that the more you relax the faster the weight loss.

And as you listen to the water gently stirring all around you, allow the sounds of the ocean to soothe you and bring your awareness to the thighs and the knees.

Notice the position of your knees now, perhaps they are a little bent or completely straight. You can try shifting around to release any cramps or stiffness that you experience here.

///

And the salty scent of the sea is penetrating your senses now, reminding you of long walks on the beach. As you steer the boat, notice the rhythmic humming of the small engine vibrating in time with your breathing. Each breath brings in more relaxation and optimises your weight loss.

///

Allow yourself to shift from doing to being, noticing how easy it is to be carried along by the water, smoothly sailing towards the deserted beach in the distance.

///

Now arriving at the hips and pelvis area. Going deep into the muscles into the joints if necessary, checking for small spots of holding and breathing into them to release them.

///

It's time to relax, truly relax, letting go of the body, letting go of the mind and allowing every limb to fall now. Allowing the body to be limp and heavy. Allowing the weight to go.

///

There is nothing for you to do right now, but let go, relax and release, as you sail effortlessly across the turquoise seas of the Caribbean.

///

And bring your awareness to the lower back now, noticing the tension held in the spine or the lower abdomen, allowing them both to expand as you breathe in deeply. Pushing them all the way out and allowing them to release and collapse fully on the exhale.

Spend a few minutes relaxing the lower back and abdomen.

///

And when you feel the release you can move your awareness up towards the upper back and chest area, and again take a deep breath in.
With the gentle waves and sound of the water encouraging you, expand the upper back and chest all the way out, filling both with clean sea air.

Clearing any negative energy that has been hanging around, letting go of any emotions that cause weight retention and allowing your body to relax fully.

Refreshing the chest, lungs and upper back with the salty sea breeze that surrounds you now. Imagine all of the stress, anxiety and extra pounds leaving with the salty sea air, let it go, let it go, let it all go.

///

And as you take in the sea air, the sun warms your head, shoulders, neck and back, allowing you to relax them, dropping the shoulders, releasing the tension in your neck, as you gently turn it from side to side, perhaps dropping the head and tucking the chin slightly.

///

And as you look ahead towards the green island that beckons you to come closer, you notice flying fish jumping on the horizon, what a sight, how exciting and joyful they seem. How playful and fun they must be.

//

As you drop your gaze, you can see all the way down to the sea bed, covered in vibrant green plants, brightly coloured coral covered in fish, large and small of every colour and description. They dart in and out, energetically, while the occasional jellyfish, lazily drift around, relaxed and at ease.

///

Imagine breathing relaxation in with every clean fresh breath, and breathing any lingering tension and excess weight out.
Following the rhythm of the waves in the water with your breathing, allowing it to ease you into a deeper state of calm and tranquillity.

///

This is the life, getting closer and closer to the white sandy beach ahead.
Feeling more and more relaxed.
Calmer and calmer.
Breathing nice and easy, soft and slow.
Surrendering lower and lower, deeper and deeper to the sounds of the Caribbean sea.

///

And finally, as your boat arrives, easing onto the shoreline, you can relax the jaw, the muscles around the eyes and the forehead and release any tension that may have returned as you prepare to explore your very own private beach.

///

As you step out of the boat, wading through the water onto the beach, you feel optimistic about the good night's sleep that awaits you. It's time to explore, this is your private island, there is nobody here to disturb you or interrupt your peace.

/

This is your private, secret place especially for you, the place where you can return whenever you need some peace and quiet, whenever you are in need of a good night's sleep.

//

And now as you walk across the warm sand, allowing the tiny grains to fall between your

toes, you see a large, well-crafted beach hut, standing majestically on four stilts.
A welcoming silhouette against the horizon.

///

And as you wade through the sand, you can enjoy the beauty of the setting sun in the distance. The pink and orange giving everything around you a warm glow.

The warm early evening sunset conspires with the gentle lapping waves of the sea and the softly swaying palm trees to create the ideal atmosphere for a good night's sleep.

And as you push forward each step heavier than the last, taking you a little deeper into the sand, each time the sand holds your feet a little longer, each time your whole body sinking a little deeper and deeper as you get closer and closer.

And finally, as you drag your tired feet, your weary body swaying in the heat, you arrive.

It's time, It's time to rest, time to put your feet up as you enter your luxury beach hut.

///

And as you climb the small steps, and enter into the ambience of pure luxury, you see the large fan that rotates effortlessly hanging from the high slanting bamboo roof. You're grateful for the cool breeze that pushes away the humid heat throughout. The cool wooden floors beneath your feet varnished and glistening add to the cool temperature as you walk.

/

You spot a hammock hanging in the corner by an open window, this will be your bed for the night. And as you climb in, you lay your head back and allow the gentle sway of the hammock to ease your weary body.

///

In the last moments of wakefulness, you allow your eyelids to close, heavy from your journey and observe the willingness of your body to completely surrender. Your mind is soothed by the sounds of the ocean waves. It's time for sleep.

And as you ease into a state of slumber, there is nothing for you to do right now but enjoy the peace and tranquillity of your private desert island.

The sounds of the Caribbean Sea in the background, erasing the stress of the day.
As you willingly let all of the pressure and tension just melt away.

///

The fan continues to create a gentle steady breeze above.
Your hammock sways back and forth. Ever so gently, back and forth, back and forth.

///

Outside of the window now the palm trees and the waves are becoming quieter and quieter as the sun sets, barely audible as you drift off.

And as you let go, drifting off, the warmth of the sun melting away any fat cells and building your muscle mass, you fall into complete relaxation, you are at peace and nature is doing its work.

Feeling totally calm and utterly relaxed, tomorrow is another day.

Night, night, and sweet dreams.

Session 5: Affirmations - Overcoming Insomnia

Overview: This affirmation session is designed to reprogram one's unconscious mind to produce a deep, restful and healthy sleep every night.

Time: 30-minutes ***[Repeat the affirmations 4 times for them to take effect in the mind of the listener.]***

[Reader Notes]

- Read the following script at a steady pace, taking your time to guide the listener with your voice.
- Allow long comfortable pauses, that you are happy with, in between passages and follow the key set out below to allow longer pauses.

[Pause Key]

... Very short pause: Reader pauses for 2 seconds

/ Short pause: Reader pauses for 10 seconds

// Medium pause: Reader pauses for 20 seconds

/// Long pause: Reader pauses for 30 seconds

[Script Begins]

Hello and welcome to this powerful affirmation session….

Affirmations are used to reprogram the unconscious beliefs and behaviours to sleep soundly and pleasantly all night.

Listening to this audio file on a daily basis can bring about tremendous positive changes.

These affirmations focus on good sleep hygiene, long-lasting healthy sleep, restful sleep and having good dreams. Listen to this audio daily for a minimum of 40 days for best results.

Relax, and enjoy!

I fall asleep easily when bedtime approaches
I sleep soundly
I sleep pleasantly
I am a deep sleeper
I am a sound sleeper
I sleep throughout the night until I wake up in the morning
I am a peaceful sleeper
I am a quiet sleeper
I am comfortable in bed
I am peaceful in bed
My mind is quiet when I am in bed
Going to sleep is easy for me
Falling asleep is easy
I sleep healthily and restfully
I sleep deeply every night
Each day as bedtime approaches I am calm
I am optimistic about falling asleep every night
Every night going to sleep is a pleasant experience
I have good dreams when I sleep

I have peaceful dreams when I sleep
My mind is silent as I fall asleep
I let go and drift into a deep sleep every night as soon as my head touches the pillow
My pillow is comfortable
My body relaxes easily and quickly when I am in bed
My mind relaxes easily and quickly when I am in bed
I let go of all unnecessary nervous tension as soon as I get into bed
I am undisturbed by light when I am asleep
I sleep easy every night
Every night sleeping is a pleasant experience
I look forward to sleeping every night
The harder I try to stay awake the drowsier I become
I start to become drowsier and drowsier as soon as I close my eyes in bed
As I close my eyes in bed my muscles begin to relax
My breathing becomes deep and calm as soon as I get into bed to fall asleep
I am positive about falling asleep easily every night

I sleep soundly all night and wake up pleasantly in the morning
I always have a restful sleep
I always have pleasant and good dreams
I am a happy sleeper
I am always energised after a good night's rest
I am relaxed when bedtime approaches
My mind and body are ready to rest in bed
Sleeping is a very natural state for me
Optimism and happy thoughts fill my dreams
I do my best to ensure my sleep environment is clean and comfortable
I choose sleep, rest, peace and relaxation
I am truly grateful that my body and mind rest easily every night
My sleep is healing
I undergo an emotional, mental and physical healing process every time I sleep
I am worthy of a good night's rest
I deserve to have a healthy restful sleep
I enjoy an undisturbed night of sleep every night

Session 6: Affirmations - Extreme fat burn

Overview: This affirmation session is designed to reprogram one's unconscious mind to burn fat faster.

Time: 30-minutes *[Repeat the affirmations 4 times for them to take effect in the mind of the listener.]*

[Reader Notes]

- Read the following script at a steady pace, taking your time to guide the listener with your voice.
- Allow long comfortable pauses, that you are happy with, in between passages and follow the key set out below to allow longer pauses.

[Pause Key]

... Very short pause: Reader pauses for 2 seconds

/ Short pause: Reader pauses for 10 seconds

// Medium pause: Reader pauses for 20 seconds

/// Long pause: Reader pauses for 30 seconds

[Script Begins]

Hello and welcome to this powerful affirmation session....

These affirmations are used to reprogram the unconscious mind to start burning fat at a faster rate.

Listening to this audio file on a daily basis can bring about tremendous positive changes.

These affirmations focus on burning fat at a faster rate by exercising more regularly. Listen to this audio daily for a minimum of 40 days for best results.

Relax, and enjoy!

I am burning fat quicker every day
I am losing weight easily
I lose more weight every day
Fat is easy to burn
I am worthy of losing weight
I am worthy of being slim
I am worthy of exercising daily
I am happy that I exercise every day
I am excited to lose weight
Burning fat is easy
Losing weight is easy
I am motivated to exercise every day
I feel like exercising every day
My fat burns faster every time I exercise
I lose my excess fat quickly and easily
Burning fat comes naturally to me
Exercising is a natural part of my daily routine
I feel bad when I skip a day of exercise
I am grateful that I enjoy exercising daily
I am grateful that I am losing more and more weight rapidly each day
I am motivated to do what it takes to burn more fat each and every day
Each and everyday I am becoming thinner and thinner

I enjoy burning more fat each day

It makes me happy to see my weight reduce

I burn more fat as I sleep

Exercise accelerates my fat burning process

My metabolism is very high

My body is a fat burning furnace

My body converts fat to energy

My body efficiently burns stored fat

My weight decreases day by day

My body responds to exercise by shedding fat

The more fat I burn the better I feel

My body wants to return to a healthy weight

Every moment of the day I am burning fat

I love the feeling of having lower body fat

I choose health over excess body fat

I burn fat efficiently and effectively

I love physical fitness

Physical fitness makes me feel empowered and amazing

Fat melts off me easily

My metabolism is at its optimal rate and it burns fat quickly

I am a physically active person

Every day I am becoming slimmer and fitter

Exercising is empowering and exciting

Everytime I sweat I burn more calories

My body is burning calories faster each day
I am losing weight every single moment
I make sure that I exercise every day without fail
I deserve to lose weight
I deserve to burn more fat every day
I am free of all obstacles that are preventing me from losing weight
I am free of all the obstacles that prevent me from exercising
My body is healthily burning every excess pound
I look forward to burning fat every day
I look forward to exercising every day
I am truly grateful that my body and mind work diligently to burn off the excess fat on my body in a healthy and natural manner

Session 7: Affirmations - Overcoming Body Anxiety

Overview: This affirmation session is designed to reprogram one's unconscious mind to overcome body anxiety.

Time: 30-minutes ***[Repeat the affirmations 4 times for them to take effect in the mind of the listener.]***

[Reader Notes]

- Read the following script at a steady pace, taking your time to guide the listener with your voice.
- Allow long comfortable pauses, that you are happy with, in between passages and follow the key set out below to allow longer pauses.

[Pause Key]

... Very short pause: Reader pauses for 2 seconds

/ Short pause: Reader pauses for 10 seconds

// Medium pause: Reader pauses for 20 seconds

/// Long pause: Reader pauses for 30 seconds

[Script Begins]

Hello and welcome to this powerful affirmation session....

These affirmations are used to reprogram the unconscious mind to start loving and appreciating your body.

Listening to this audio file on a daily basis can bring about tremendous positive changes.

These affirmations focus on overcoming body anxiety by working on loving and appreciating your body. Listen to this audio daily for a minimum of 40 days for best results.

Relax, and enjoy!

I am beautiful
I love my body
I am becoming thinner and thinner
I enjoy looking at my body
I am comfortable in my own body
I am comfortable in my skin
I am grateful for my body
I am worthy of becoming my ideal weight
My body is beautiful
My inner beauty shines forth daily
Every day I give thanks for my body
I appreciate and give love to all parts of my body
I am pretty
I feel beautiful
I feel in love with my body
I give my body the attention that it requires
I give my body the care that it needs
I look after my body

Giving love to my body is important to me
Giving thanks to my body is important to me
I am proud of who I am
I love myself
I am confident about my body
I am confident about myself
I believe in myself
I believe I can transform my body
I enjoy giving thanks to my body
I praise my body
I am connected to my body
I am in sync with my body
I care deeply about the health of my body
I do my best to look after my body every day
I say loving things about my body
I think loving thoughts about my body
I am comfortable being in my body in public
I enjoy being appreciated
I enjoy being beautiful
I am thankful that I am beautiful
I am thankful that I feel beautiful
I am impressed with the progress of my body every day
I am thankful I work hard to improve my body
I am motivated to love my body more and more

I am motivated to transform my body
I work hard to ensure my body is healthy and loved
My love for my body is so strong that other people can feel it
I am so comfortable and confident within myself that other people compliment me
I compliment my body
I am comfortable being me
I am truly empowered to love and accept my body
I appreciate every part of my body
I am grateful that I accept my body fully and completely
I am perfect and complete just the way I am
My body is a vessel for my ultimate potential
Being whole and grounded makes me beautiful
I deserve to be treated with love and respect
I deserve to be beautiful
I deserve to be loved for who I am
I trust the wisdom of my body
My body is an amazing gift, I treat it with love and respect

Conclusion

Thank you for listening
Find more help @ _____

www.ingramcontent.com/pod-product-compliance
Lightning Source LLC
Chambersburg PA
CBHW072200100526
44589CB00015B/2299